MISSISSIPPI

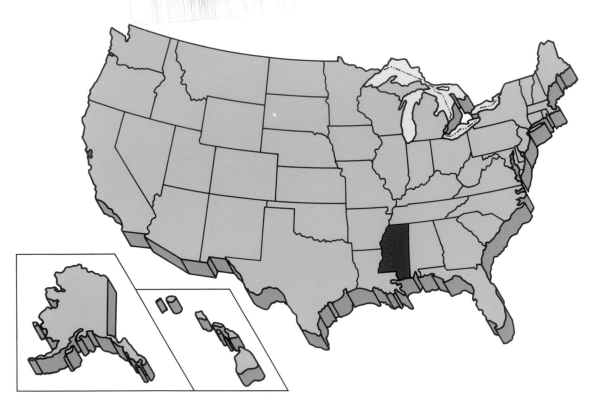

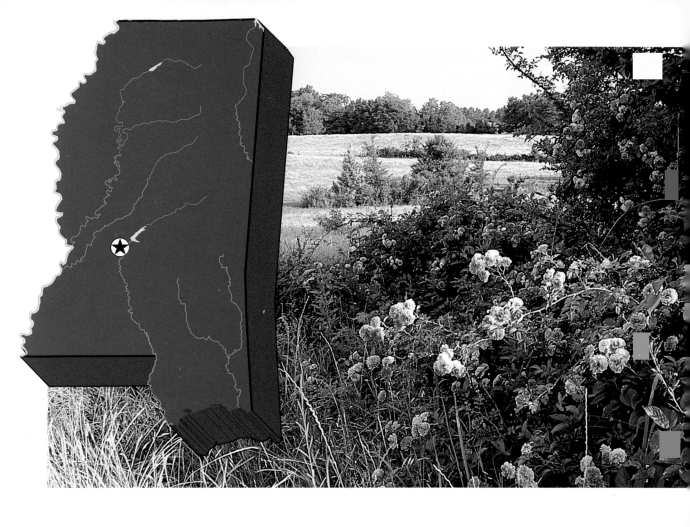

Hello U.S.A.

MISSISSIPPI

Anna Ready

Lerner Publications Company

LIBRARY OF CONGRESS
CATALOGING-IN-PUBLICATION DATA
Ready, Anna.
    Mississippi / Anna Ready.
        p.   cm. — (Hello U.S.A.)
    Includes index.
    Summary: Introduces the geography, history,
people, and environmental issues of Mississippi.
    ISBN 0-8225-2743-X (lib. bdg.)
    1. Mississippi—Juvenile literature.
[1. Mississippi.] I. Title. II. Series.
F341.3.R43   1993
976.2—dc20   92-31056
                                         CIP
                                          AC

Cover photograph of *The Golden Fisherman*—a
sculpture in downtown Biloxi, Mississippi—by
Frederica Georgia.

The glossary that begins on page 68 gives defini-
tions of words shown in **bold type** in the text.

Manufactured in the United States of America

1   2   3   4   5   6   98   97   96   95   94   93

 This book is printed on
acid-free, recyclable paper.

CONTENTS

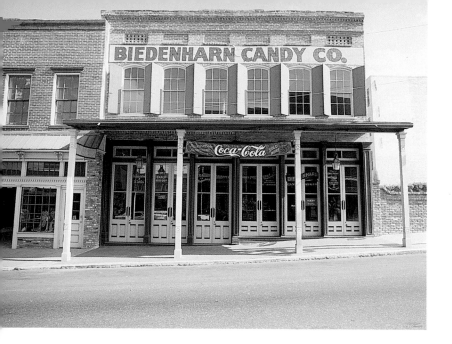

The Biedenharn Candy Company was the birthplace of bottled Coca-Cola.

Did You Know . . . ?

❑ Coca-Cola was first bottled in 1894 in Vicksburg, Mississippi. Joseph A. Biedenharn of the Biedenharn Candy Company poured the popular beverage into bottles so it could be delivered to rural, or country, areas that didn't have their own soda fountains.

❑ Elvis Presley, a singer who became famous as the King of Rock and Roll, was born in Tupelo, Mississippi, on January 8, 1935.

❑ More upholstered (padded and covered) furniture comes from Mississippi than from any other state in the country.

❑ Mississippi's state bird, the mockingbird, is a copycat. The small gray bird imitates all sorts of noises, from playing pianos to barking dogs.

❑ Mississippi is sometimes called the Mud-Cat State for the many catfish that feed near the muddy bottoms of the state's waterways.

A Trip Around the State

The Magnolia State. Mississippi's nickname comes from a beautiful evergreen tree with sweet-smelling white flowers. Magnolias grow throughout the state, which boasts natural beauty ranging from lush forests to white, sandy beaches to the wide waters of the Mississippi, the river from which the state takes its name.

Mississippi is a southern state. Its neighbors are Tennessee, Alabama, Louisiana, and Arkansas. The Mississippi River, which empties into the Gulf of Mexico, forms most of the state's western border. Part of the Atlantic Ocean, the Gulf of Mexico washes up against Mississippi's southern coast. A series of small islands called the Gulf Islands National Seashore lies just off the shore.

The magnolia is Mississippi's state flower.

9

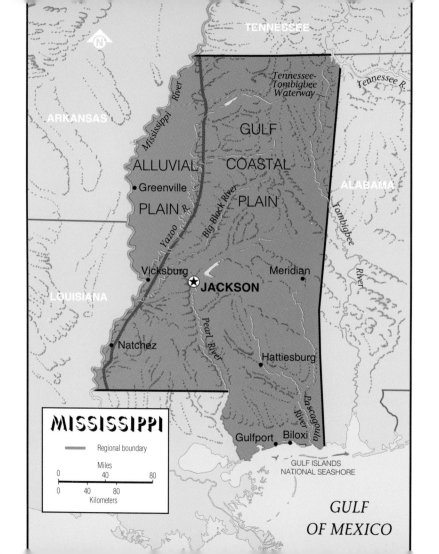

Many rivers flow through Mississippi's two land regions. Built across some of the rivers, dams back up water and slow it down, forming reservoirs (artificial lakes). In fact, the state's largest lakes are reservoirs.

Mississippi's land slopes gently downward from its highest point in the north to sea level at the Gulf of Mexico. The state is divided into two regions—the Alluvial Plain and the Gulf Coastal Plain.

The soil of the Alluvial Plain, a narrow strip of land along the western edge of the state, is rich and deep. Over time, the region's many rivers have flooded and deposited **alluvium**—a fertile mixture of fine dirt, clay, sand, and gravel —along their banks. This area of soil enriched by river flooding is known as a **delta**. In fact, most Mississippians refer to the Alluvial Plain as the Delta. Cotton and soybeans grow very well here.

The sky over the Mississippi Delta glows with the colors of the setting sun.

The Gulf Coastal Plain extends from the Delta to the eastern edge of the state. The Tennessee River Hills rise in the northeastern corner of the coastal plain. The tallest of these hills reaches 806 feet (246 meters) and is the highest point in the state. At the southern end of the coastal plain region, the Piney Woods are home to loblolly, longleaf, and slash pine trees.

Lowlands and **prairies,** or grasslands, are also part of the Gulf Coastal Plain. Farmers grow corn and hay in the rich, dark soil of the Black Belt, the region's largest prairie. Cattle graze on the Black Belt's grasses.

The Mississippi River is the state's most important waterway. In fact, *Mississippi* means "great water" or "big river" in the language of the American Indians who lived near the river long ago. Smaller rivers such as the Big Black and the Yazoo flow westward into the Mississippi. The Pearl, Pascagoula, and Tombigbee rivers flow into the Gulf.

Colorful bluffs *(above)* rise in southeastern Mississippi, where loblolly *(facing page)* and other kinds of pine trees thrive.

Winters in Mississippi are mild, with only occasional snow and ice.

Mississippi's climate is warm and moist. The average rainfall in the north is more than 50 inches (130 centimeters). Even more rain falls in the southeastern part of the state near the Gulf. Occasionally, northern Mississippians see snow, but it usually doesn't stay on the ground for long.

Winters are short and mild, with average temperatures of about 46° F (8° C). Winds off the Gulf of Mexico cool the state in the summertime, when the average temperature is about 81° F (27° C). During the late summer and early fall, violent storms called hurricanes sometimes blow in from the Gulf of Mexico. The storms' heavy rains, high waves, and strong winds can cause serious damage to towns along the coast.

A girl feeds Canada geese spending the winter in Mississippi.

Spanish moss, a plant without roots, hangs from a live oak tree.

Mississippi's warm, wet climate, as well as its rich soil, helps flowering shrubs such as azaleas, camellias, and dogwoods grow throughout the state. More than 100 kinds of trees grow in the state's forests. Woodlands cover nearly two-thirds of the state, where pecan, palm, cottonwood, tupelo, live oak, and pine trees thrive.

Mississippi's forests are home to many animals, including deer, foxes, opossums, rabbits, squirrels, quail, and wild turkeys. An adventurous hiker walking through the woods might spot an alligator swimming in a pond. Anglers catch bass, bream, and catfish in the state's many rivers. In the waters of the Gulf, fishers haul in shrimp, crabs, and oysters.

Like box turtles *(left)*, **alligators** *(above)*
live on land and in water.

Mississippi's Story

Long ago no one lived in what is now Mississippi. Its land was rich and forested. Far to the north, an icy land bridge stretched between Asia and North America.

More than 20,000 years ago, hunters from Asia followed wild animals across the land bridge. As thousands of years passed, groups of people migrated, or wandered, farther and farther south. By A.D. 700, some of the descendants of these people, known as American Indians, or Native Americans, were living in villages in the region now known as Mississippi.

These Indians, called mound builders, buried their dead in big pits. Layers of dirt were piled on top of the pits to form giant mounds. Priests and chiefs lived on special mounds built just for them. Villagers lived in houses near these mounds.

No one knows exactly what happened to the mound builders, but by 1500 most of them had disappeared. At this time, tribes of Natchez, Choctaw, and Chickasaw Indians—all of whom were probably related to the mound builders—were living in villages on the eastern banks of the Mississippi River. Many smaller tribes also lived in this fertile region of what is now Mississippi.

Thousands of years ago, American Indians built giant mounds *(above)* **in Mississippi. Some mounds served as burial sites, while others were places of worship** *(inset).*

Hundreds of players compete in a game of lacrosse, a popular sport played by the Choctaw and other Indian tribes.

The largest and most powerful tribe was the Natchez, who lived near what became Natchez, Mississippi. These Indians were skilled at making cloth and pottery. For food the Natchez planted corn, melons, squash, and beans. They hunted deer and caught fish. Like their ancestors, they also built mounds.

The Natchez divided their society into different groups. At the top was the king, called the Great Sun, and his family. At the bottom were common people, called Stinkards, who did the hard work of farming and mound building.

The Choctaw lived in the south central part of what is now Mississippi. They planted crops and built canoes for fishing, hunting, and trading trips. The Choctaw, like many other Indian tribes, played lacrosse, a ball game in which players try to score a goal by using a special racket to carry and pass a ball.

The Chickasaw lived in what would become northern Mississippi. Each village was run by a chief. Like the Choctaw and the Natchez, the Chickasaw farmed and fished for food. They also raised cattle.

In 1541 Hernando de Soto became the first European to reach the Mississippi River.

By the 1540s, between 25,000 and 35,000 American Indians were living in present-day Mississippi. At that time, they encountered the first Europeans to visit the area. Searching for gold, Spanish explorer Hernando de Soto and his army passed through Chickasaw territory and demanded that the Indians carry supplies for the Spanish.

The Chickasaw refused. In the battle that followed, many Native Americans and several Spaniards were killed. De Soto and his army left the area without finding gold.

Indians in the region did not see another white person for another 100 years. In 1682 French explorer René-Robert Cavelier de La Salle traveled all the way down the Mississippi River to the Gulf of Mexico. He claimed the entire river valley—including what is now Mississippi—for France. The explorer named the region Louisiana after Louis XIV, the king of France.

When French explorer La Salle reached the point where the Mississippi River flows into the Gulf of Mexico, he put up a cross, claiming the entire river valley for France.

23

Soon more Europeans began to arrive in what is now Mississippi. In 1698 British traders came to the area. By 1716 the French had established two settlements in the region—one near Biloxi and the other at Natchez. The British and the French traded cloth, guns, beads, and knives with the Indians in exchange for animal furs. The furs were then sold in Europe for a huge profit.

In the early 1700s, the French shipped people from West Africa to what is now Mississippi to work as slaves on rice and tobacco farms.

The Natchez Revolt

The French were the first Europeans to settle along the Mississippi River in southwestern Mississippi. At first the French got along well with the American Indians living in the area. In 1716 Natchez Indians even helped the French build Fort Rosalie, a trading post and fort overlooking the Mississippi River near Natchez. But no one imagined that a war between the Natchez and the French would soon break out.

As French settlers came to the area, they gradually claimed more and more of the fertile land that belonged to the Natchez. In 1729 the French governor of the Mississippi River valley decided to build a large farm right on the site of the Natchez Indians' main village. He ordered all the Indians to leave at once. But the Natchez didn't want to lose any more of their land. They decided to fight for their village and attacked Fort Rosalie and other French settlements along the Mississippi River. The French army struck back and by 1731 had killed almost every member of the tribe. The few surviving Indians either settled with other tribes in the region or were sold into slavery. With this war, called the Natchez Revolt, the Natchez tribe was destroyed forever.

Both France and Great Britain claimed a lot of land in North America. The more land they controlled, the more money they could make from the fur trade. Between 1754 and 1763, the two nations fought over who would control the most land in North America.

During this conflict—known as the French and Indian War—the Choctaw sided with the French and the Chickasaw sided with the British. When Great Britain won the war, it gained control of most of France's North American land claims, including what is now Mississippi.

But British rule did not last long. After Great Britain lost the American Revolution in 1783, Mis-

When Mississippi became a U.S. territory in 1798, Natchez—an important river town—became its capital.

sissippi became a territory of the United States. And on December 10, 1817, Mississippi was admitted to the Union as the 20th state.

The Devil's Backbone

One of Mississippi's most important highways was the Natchez Trace, an overland route stretching nearly 500 miles (800 km) from Natchez, Mississippi, to Nashville, Tennessee. Herds of buffalo originally beat the path through the woods thousands of years ago. For many years, Indians in central Tennessee depended on the trail to get to the Mississippi River, where they traded with local tribes.

The Natchez Trace was a busy road. In the late 1700s and early 1800s, white settlers from the east followed the ancient overland route to Mississippi. Traders used the trail, too. And starting in 1800, the U.S. government began using the Natchez Trace as the postal route to Mississippi and Louisiana.

But the trail was dangerous. Along the way, a traveler had to walk through dense forests in all kinds of weather and be prepared to wade through swamps and swim across rivers. Wild animals and poisonous snakes were common. So were fierce outlaws who waited to steal from or even kill travelers. Because of these hazards, the Natchez Trace became known as the Devil's Backbone.

In the early 1820s, travelers deserted the Natchez Trace in favor of steamboats, which could safely travel the mighty Mississippi River. In 1938 the U.S. government established the Natchez Trace Parkway to preserve the Devil's Backbone for generations to come.

In the late 1700s and early 1800s, white settlers from more crowded states in the east began to move to Mississippi to farm its rich land. Neither the settlers nor the U.S. government cared that the land belonged to American Indians. The U.S. government thought it had its own right to the land, so it forced the Choctaw and the Chickasaw to sign **treaties.** By signing these documents, the two tribes agreed to give up all their land in the state of Mississippi.

During the 1830s, the U.S. Army forced most of the Choctaw and the Chickasaw to leave Mississippi. The Indians were sent to the Indian Territory in what is now Oklahoma. During the long march west, thousands of Native Americans died from disease and lack of food and water. Because of all the suffering, this forced march is called the Trail of Tears.

In the 1830s, the Choctaw and Chickasaw Indians were forced to leave their homelands in Mississippi. They walked the Trail of Tears to their new homes in what is now Oklahoma.

During the next 30 years, some of Mississippi's white settlers grew quite rich growing cotton on very large farms called **plantations**. Black people—who had been brought to America from Africa by slave traders—were forced to do the backbreaking work of planting and harvesting. By 1860 black slaves made up more than half of Mississippi's population.

Many of the biggest plantations were close to the Mississippi River. Cotton grew well in the rich soil

At docks along the Mississippi River, planters loaded bales of cotton onto steamboats headed for Northern markets, where the cotton was sold to mills and made into cloth.

along the banks of the river, and plantation owners could easily load their harvest onto steamboats, which carried the crop to market. Prices for cotton were high, and Mississippi became one of the richest states in the country.

But Northern states had outlawed slavery, and they wanted Southern states to do the same. Southerners protested. Without slavery, many Southern plantation owners felt they would no longer be able to earn enough money. To protect the interests of their state, Mississippians left the Union in 1861, joining other Southern states to form the Confederate States of America (the Confederacy).

Jefferson Davis, a planter and U.S. senator from Mississippi, became the president of the Confederacy in February 1861. Just two months later, the Civil War broke out. About 80,000 Mississippians fought for the Confederacy during this bloody war between the North and the South.

Jefferson Davis, president of the Confederacy, knew that by leaving the Union, Southern states risked going to war against the Northern states.

Union troops dug temporary shelters into hillsides during the 47-day Siege of Vicksburg.

Mississippi was the site of about 500 battles during the Civil War. The most important battle in the state was fought in 1863 at Vicksburg, near the Mississippi River. For 47 days, the Northern army bombed the city, hoping to gain control of this important river town. To escape the bombing, residents hid in hillside caves, which were crowded and filled with mosquitoes. With little food and few supplies left, the Southern army had to give up.

Almost two years later, the North won the Civil War. Afterward, Mississippians went through a difficult period called **Reconstruction,** when residents worked to rebuild their state. Houses, barns, railroads, crops, and livestock had been destroyed during the war. Most people were very poor.

33

During Reconstruction, Mississippi had to follow certain laws to get back into the Union. Many of the new laws had to do with the rights of African Americans, who were freed from slavery after the war. Black men were given the right to vote and were allowed to run for political office.

After the war, plantation owners

began looking for new ways to farm their land. Without slaves—who had worked for no wages—plantation owners turned instead to **sharecropping**. In the sharecropping system, plantation owners provided seeds and tools to farmers, called sharecroppers, who worked only a small piece of the land. After the harvest, sharecroppers had to give most of the crops to the plantation owner.

The main crop in Mississippi was still cotton, but prices for this crop were very low after the war. Because plantation owners got most of the money from the harvest, sharecroppers struggled to make a living.

In 1870 the U.S. government allowed Mississippi to rejoin the Union. But many white Mississippians did not want former slaves to have the same rights as whites. Some joined the Ku Klux Klan, a group of white people who threatened and killed black people. Klan members hoped that their actions would scare African Americans into giving up their rights.

After the Civil War, many Mississippians lived on small farms *(facing page)* **and were very poor.**

Mississippi's state flag, which became official in 1894, honors both the Confederacy and the Union. In the upper left corner is the Confederate battle flag. The red, white, and blue stripes covering the rest of the flag are the colors of the U.S. flag.

In 1890 Mississippi made new laws that prevented blacks from voting. Blacks were also not allowed to attend the same schools as whites. They couldn't use the same bathrooms, hotel rooms, schools, or drinking fountains. And, without the right to vote, black Mississippians could not change these laws.

At the beginning of the 1900s, many Mississippians were still poor. The state earned most of its money from cotton, but prices for the crop were still very low. During the 1930s, many people left Mississippi to try to look for better jobs in other states.

To help bring different kinds of jobs and more money to the state, Mississippi's government started a program in 1936 to help build factories in Mississippi. Thousands of new jobs were created, many of them in shipbuilding.

The discovery of oil at Tinsley in 1939 brought more new jobs to Mississippi. And during World War II (1939–1945), factories near Flora and Aberdeen began producing weapons. Shipbuilding boomed in Pascagoula. Military training camps and airfields sprang up throughout the state.

During World War II, many women in Mississippi got jobs making weapons in factories.

After the war, African Americans began a new fight for equal rights called the **civil rights movement.** In 1954 the U.S. Supreme Court ruled that black students and white students should be allowed to attend the same public schools.

Eight years later, in 1962, a black Mississippian named James Meredith tried to enroll at the all-white University of Mississippi.

Civil rights marchers greet field-workers in Mississippi.

James Meredith was the first African American to register for classes at the University of Mississippi.

A large group of white people gathered to protest. Violence broke out, and two people were killed. Meredith enrolled, but U.S. government troops stayed at the university to protect him until he graduated in 1963.

In 1965 Mississippi's black citizens again won the right to vote. Many African Americans in Mississippi voted for the first time in their lives. And in 1969, the citizens of Fayette elected Charles Evers—the first black mayor in Mississippi since Reconstruction.

By 1970 more Mississippians were working in factories than on farms. But many of these factory jobs pay low wages. Compared to other states, Mississippi is poor.

18,000 B.C. Ancient hunters come to North America from Asia

A.D. 700 Mound builders live in the region now called Mississippi

1541 Hernando de Soto explores northern Mississippi

1682 La Salle claims the Mississippi River valley for France

1729 Natchez Revolt

1798 Mississippi becomes a U.S. territory

But Mississippi is a state on the move. The Tennessee-Tombigbee Waterway, which passes through Mississippi on its way to the Gulf of Mexico, has brought many new jobs to the state. Opened in 1985, the waterway gives the state's industries a quick and inexpensive route for shipping goods to ports on the Gulf. Projects like this make Mississippians proud of their state and hopeful for its future.

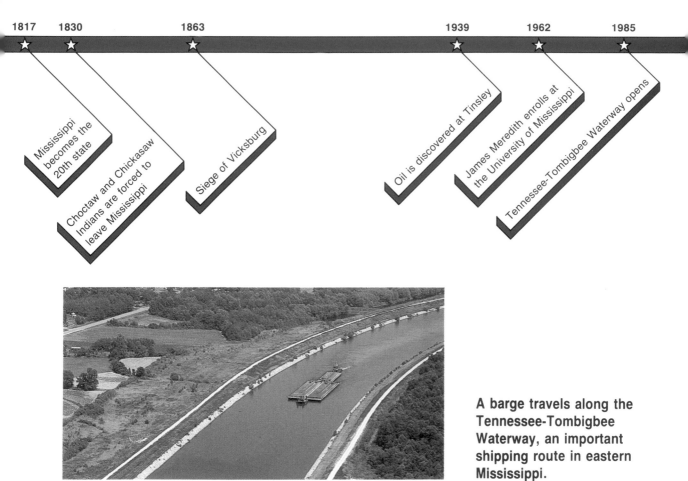

1817 — Mississippi becomes the 20th state

1830 — Choctaw and Chickasaw Indians are forced to leave Mississippi

1863 — Siege of Vicksburg

1939 — Oil is discovered at Tinsley

1962 — James Meredith enrolls at the University of Mississippi

1985 — Tennessee-Tombigbee Waterway opens

A barge travels along the Tennessee-Tombigbee Waterway, an important shipping route in eastern Mississippi.

41

Living and Working in Mississippi

Native Americans and pioneers once made their way to Mississippi by traveling along the Natchez Trace or boating down the Mississippi River. People lived in villages, on farms, or in small towns. Nowadays, airports and highways link Mississippi to the rest of the country, and cities and industries are growing. For this reason, many Mississippians call their state the State of Change.

A grandfather and grandson enjoy a sunny afternoon together.

About 13,000 Asian Americans live in Mississippi.

Mississippi is home to 2.6 million people. Nearly two out of every three residents are white people. The ancestors of most Mississippians came to the United States from Great Britain, France, and other European countries.

About one out of every three Mississippi residents is African American. Almost all black Mississippians were born in the United States and can trace their roots back to Africa. Asian Americans, Latinos, and American Indians total less than 1 percent of the population.

When the U.S. government moved Indians west in the 1830s, about 5,000 Choctaw Indians refused to leave their homeland in

Mississippi's capitol building is in Jackson.

Mississippi. Some of their descendants now live on the Choctaw Reservation, land in east central Mississippi that the government reserved for these Indians. Nearby is Nanih Waiya, a mound that the Choctaw believe is the birthplace of their people.

Almost half of Mississippi's residents live in cities. Many of the Mississippians who live in rural areas drive to work in nearby cities. Mississippi's largest cities are Biloxi, Greenville, Hattiesburg, Meridian, Gulfport, and Jackson— the state capital.

45

A young Choctaw girl wears colorful beadwork.

Communities throughout Mississippi host many festivals during the year. The Choctaw celebrate their heritage at the Choctaw Indian Fair held each July in Philadelphia. In nearby Jackson, the State Fair draws many people in the fall, as does the Sweet Potato Festival in Vardaman. The town of Biloxi holds a shrimp festival each June to celebrate the beginning of the shrimp-fishing season. Townspeople crown a shrimp queen and bless the fishing boats.

Visitors to Mississippi find many different kinds of music in the state. One of the most popular musical events is the Delta Blues Festival, held each fall in Greenville. Fans of country music enjoy performances by country-western singers at the Jimmie Rodgers Festival, which takes place in Meridian each spring.

With its mild climate, Mississippi is a great place to be outdoors. Miles of white, sandy beaches attract sunbathers to the Gulf coast year-round. The Tennessee-Tombigbee Waterway is a good place for boating and waterskiing. And many people enjoy hiking the nature trails along the Natchez Trace Parkway.

In the summer, Mississippians enjoy hot-air balloon races (above) **in Corinth. Waterskiing** (right) **on the state's many waterways is also popular.**

47

Natchez is a good place to see mansions such as Longwood, which was built before the Civil War.

History buffs can try to imagine what plantation life was like before the Civil War at mansions in Vicksburg, Natchez, and Columbus. Guides dressed in clothes in the style of the 1800s lead tours through these homes. At Florewood River Plantation near Greenwood, visitors can also see how crops were planted and harvested in the 1800s.

Those who want to learn more about Native American history can visit Grand Village of the Natchez Indians, a model of a Natchez village. Nearby is Emerald Mound. Built about 1,000 years ago by mound-building Indians, Emerald is the third largest mound in the United States. And Winterville Mounds in Greenville is the site of more mounds than in almost any area of the Mississippi River valley.

Many working Mississippians help tourists enjoy their vacation in the state. These workers, including hotel clerks and park rangers, have what are called service jobs. In fact, more than half of all working Mississippians have some kind of service job, helping either people or businesses. Service workers in Mississippi teach, sell cars, work in department stores and restaurants, sell houses and office space, and work for the government.

Mississippi's teachers help students learn computer skills.

One out of every four working people in Mississippi has a manufacturing job. Mississippi's forests supply lumber for making plywood, paper products, boxes, and furniture. Other manufacturers in the state make stereos, telephones, chemicals, plastics, and clothing. Workers also package meat and shrimp. And Pascagoula is still an important center for shipbuilding.

Industries in Mississippi that support U.S. space programs are growing. Workers are building a factory in northeastern Mississippi that will produce rocket motors for space shuttles. The motors will then be transported down the Tennessee-Tombigbee Waterway to be tested at the John C. Stennis Space Center on the Gulf coast.

Barges on the Tennessee-Tombigbee Waterway transport logs to mills where the wood is sawed into lumber or ground up to make paper products.

Workers *(inset)* **place a space-shuttle engine on a special stand** *(above)* **for testing at the John C. Stennis Space Center.**

Farmers use machines to pick cotton. The load is then taken to a cotton gin, which cleans the cotton and packs it into giant bales.

Agriculture is no longer as important as it once was in Mississippi. But farmers still grow cotton, and soybeans are also a major crop. Pecans, sweet potatoes, cucumbers, peaches, watermelons, and grapes are grown in Mississippi too. Many farmers raise chickens and beef and dairy cattle.

Very few of Mississippi's workers—only 1 percent—have jobs in mining. Workers dig for limestone, clay, and sand and gravel. But petroleum and natural gas earn more money for the state than other minerals.

Mississippi earns millions of dollars from fishing. Shrimp is the most important catch, but fishers also bring in oysters, red snapper, and menhaden. And Mississippi's fish farmers raise more catfish each year than any other state in the country.

Many Mississippians depend on the Gulf of Mexico to earn a living. Some people catch shrimp (above) **in its waters, while others drill for oil at huge offshore platforms** (left).

Protecting the Environment

With more than 17 million acres (6.9 million hectares) of forestland, wood is one of Mississippi's most important natural resources. Many people in the state earn a living by chopping down some of these trees, working in sawmills, or making wood products such as furniture and paper.

Mississippi's forests *(facing page)* **are important to the state's economy. Using big machines** *(inset)*, **workers cut down trees and sort them into piles that can be easily transported to sawmills.**

Some people use wood for fuel to keep warm and to cook with, both at home and on camping trips. But the process of burning wood and manufacturing some wood products can produce a dangerous chemical called **dioxin,** which is harmful to the environment. Sources of dioxin include fireplaces, wood-burning stoves, and forest fires. Garbage-burning plants and factories that make certain kinds of chemicals that kill insects and weeds are also sources of dioxin. But the main source of dioxin in Mississippi is paper mills.

Paper mills make paper by cutting up logs into chips. The chips are mixed with chemicals and cooked at high temperatures to produce pulp, a soft, woody material. The pulp is washed and then bleached with chlorine to make sure the paper will be white and long-lasting. During the bleaching process—when wood, chlorine, and heat combine—dioxin is produced.

The wet, bleached pulp is then spread out on large screens and passed between rollers to squeeze out all the water. Paper mills produce millions of gallons of this wastewater, which is contaminated with dioxin. Water treatment plants in cities and towns are unable to handle this amount of wastewater, so the mills must apply for government permits to empty their wastewater into nearby rivers and streams. The government limits the amount of dioxin that can be emptied into waterways, but the chemical still ends up in the state's rivers and streams.

Logs *(left)* **are ground up at mills** *(below)* **to be made into paper products such as towels, tissues, and writing paper.**

Gate No. 3

If eaten regularly, fish contaminated with dioxin can cause health problems in humans.

When dioxin enters the waterways, it pollutes not only the water but also the plants and animals in the water. Fish become contaminated from eating the poisoned plants. Over time, fish build up a lot of dioxin in their systems.

Scientists have found that dioxin causes birth defects and cancer in animals. The U.S. Environmental Protection Agency (EPA) believes that dioxin can cause cancer in human beings, too. Mississippi's leaders are worried that people who regularly eat fish from the state's rivers will develop cancer.

Over the past several years, Mississippi has performed a series of tests to see how much dioxin is in the state's rivers and fish. When researchers studied fish in some rivers in southeastern Mississippi, they discovered that the amount of dioxin in certain fish was above the level the EPA thinks is safe.

Because of these studies, Mississippi urges people not to eat any fish from a river that has tested high in dioxin. People are also warned to eat only small fish and to avoid larger, older fish, which have had a longer time to consume and to build up the chemical in their systems.

Mississippi warns people of the dangers of dioxin by posting signs along rivers polluted with the chemical.

Mississippians want to keep
their waterways clean and
safe for future generations.

Some of Mississippi's paper mills are helping, too, by paying for ongoing studies of the state's rivers. Some mills are also trying new methods of bleaching pulp to help reduce the amount of dioxin that is produced during the bleaching process.

But some people aren't worried about dioxin. They think that the government has exaggerated the dangers of dioxin. They believe that even if people were to eat fish every day, they wouldn't be able to eat enough dioxin to develop cancer. And some mill owners are reluctant to change the way they bleach pulp. New methods are very expensive and no one knows for sure how much safer they are.

But the state of Mississippi continues to be cautious. Researchers are still studying the levels of dioxin in the state's waterways. Signs along contaminated rivers warn people that the fish they catch could be harmful to their health. These steps will help protect residents and the environment. Looking for ways to reduce and prevent dioxin pollution is an important goal for Mississippians.

Mississippi's Famous People

◀ MEDGAR EVERS

▲ CHARLES EVERS

ACTIVISTS

Charles Evers (born 1922) and **Medgar Evers** (1925–1963) were born in Decatur, Mississippi. The two brothers encouraged African Americans to vote and to stand up for equal rights. In 1963 Medgar was shot and killed. In 1969 residents of Fayette, Mississippi, elected Charles the first black mayor in Mississippi since Reconstruction. He served four terms.

Emmett York (1903–1971) started the Choctaw High School in Pearl River, Mississippi, in 1963. He also set up the United Southeastern Tribes, a council dedicated to helping Indians in Mississippi. York was born in Standing Pine, Mississippi.

◀ EMMETT YORK

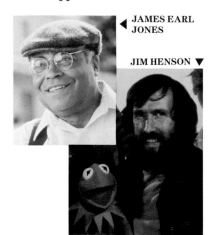

◀ JAMES EARL JONES

JIM HENSON ▼

ACTORS & ENTERTAINERS

Jim Henson (1936–1990), of Greenville, Mississippi, created a collection of puppets known as the Muppets. In 1955 Henson made his first puppet, Kermit the Frog, using his mother's old spring coat and a Ping-Pong ball. Henson later made Big Bird, the Cookie Monster, and other characters for the television show "Sesame Street." The large collection of Muppets has also starred in three movies.

James Earl Jones (born 1931) is an actor from Arkabutla, Mississippi. Known for his clear, deep voice, Jones was the voice of Darth Vader in the *Star Wars* films. The actor has appeared in many films and plays and has won Tony awards for his performances in the plays *The Great White Hope* and *Fences*.

Oprah Winfrey (born 1954) is an actress and talk-show host from Kosciusko, Mississippi. The "Oprah Winfrey Show" has become one of the most widely viewed daytime shows on television. Winfrey has also starred in films including *The Color Purple* and *Native Son*.

▲ OPRAH WINFREY

ATHLETES

▲ WALTER PAYTON

▲ DAVE PARKER

◀ JERRY RICE

Spencer Haywood (born 1949) is a two-time all-star basketball player from Silver City, Mississippi. Haywood was a member of the U. S. Olympic team in 1968 and went on to play professionally for 14 years with six different teams.

Dave Parker (born 1951) has played professional baseball with several different teams. The outfielder won the National League's batting title in 1977 and 1978. Parker, from Jackson, was also named the league's Most Valuable Player in 1978.

Walter Payton (born 1954) holds the record for rushing in a career, running a total of almost 17,000 yards (15,545 m) in 13 seasons. The running back, who played with the Chicago Bears, was named the National Football League's Most Valuable Player in 1977 and 1978. Payton is from Columbia, Mississippi.

Jerry Rice (born 1962), of Crawford, Mississippi, is a wide receiver for the San Francisco 49ers football team. In 1987 Rice caught a record 22 touchdown passes, scored 138 points, and was named the National Football League's Most Valuable Player, an honor he received again in 1990.

BUSINESS LEADER

Robert Pittman (born 1953) created MTV, a cable music network, in 1981. Since then, MTV has grown to include several programs, a library with more than 8,000 videos, and viewers in countries throughout the world. Pittman was born in Jackson.

◄ ROBERT PITTMAN

JOHN ▼ LEE HOOKER

MUSICIANS

Bo Diddley (born 1928) is from McComb, Mississippi. A blues singer and songwriter, Diddley is best known for his song "I'm Sorry." The musician plays the guitar, harmonica, trombone, and violin.

John Lee Hooker (born 1917) is a blues singer, songwriter, and guitar player from Clarksdale, Mississippi. His first musical instrument was nothing more than an inner tube played on a barn door. Hooker is now considered a legend among blues musicians.

◄ B. B. KING

▲ MUDDY WATERS

B. B. King (born 1925) is from Indianola, Mississippi. One of the best-known blues musicians of all time, King sings and plays the guitar and the clarinet. King's first initials come from an old stage name, the Blues Boy.

McKinley ("Muddy Waters") Morganfield (1915–1983) was a well-known blues singer from Rolling Fork, Mississippi. The musician also played the guitar and the harmonica. Morganfield's grandmother gave him his famous nickname because as a young boy he liked to play in a local creek.

▼ TAMMY WYNETTE

LEONTYNE PRICE ▶

Leontyne Price (born 1927), an opera singer from Laurel, Mississippi, has starred in operas all over the world. The famous soprano has performed at the White House, at presidential inaugurations, and even for the Pope. Price is also a recording artist who has won 20 Grammy Awards.

Tammy Wynette (born 1942) is an award-winning country music singer. She was named female vocalist of the year by the Country Music Association in 1968, 1969, and 1970. Wynette is from Tupelo, Mississippi.

WRITERS

WILLIAM FAULKNER ▶

▼ EUDORA WELTY

RICHARD WRIGHT ▶

William Faulkner (1897–1962) lived most of his life in Oxford, Mississippi. The author wrote many short stories and novels, including *The Sound and the Fury* and *As I Lay Dying.* In 1949 Faulkner won the Nobel Prize for literature. He also won Pulitzer Prizes in 1955 and 1963.

Eudora Welty (born 1909) is a writer of short stories, novels, essays, and reviews. She won a Pulitzer Prize in 1973 for *The Optimist's Daughter.* Welty is from Jackson.

Tennessee Williams (1911–1983) was born in Columbus, Mississippi. He won Pulitzer Prizes for the classic plays *A Streetcar Named Desire* and *Cat on a Hot Tin Roof,* both of which were made into movies.

Richard Wright (1908–1960) was one of the country's leading African American authors in the 1940s. He is best known for his novels *Native Son* and *Black Boy,* although he also wrote poetry and essays. Wright was born near Natchez.

Facts-at-a-Glance

Nickname: Magnolia State
Song: "Go, Mississippi"
Motto: *Virtute et Armis* (By Valor and Arms)
Flower: magnolia
Tree: magnolia
Bird: mockingbird

Population: 2,573,216*
Rank in population, nationwide: 31st
Area: 48,434 sq mi (125,444 sq km)
Rank in area, nationwide: 32nd
Date and ranking of statehood:
  December 10, 1817, the 20th state
Capital: Jackson
Major cities (and populations*):
  Jackson (196,637), Biloxi (46,319),
  Greenville (45,226), Hattiesburg (41,882),
  Meridian (41,036)
U.S. senators: 2
U.S. representatives: 5
Electoral votes: 7

Places to visit: Elvis Presley's birthplace in Tupelo, Florewood River Plantation near Greenwood, Natchez Trace Parkway headquartered in Tupelo, Petrified Forest National Park near Flora, Vicksburg National Military Park in Vicksburg

Annual events: Spring Pilgrimage in Natchez (March–April), World Catfish Festival in Belzoni (April), Watermelon Festival in Mize (July), Delta Blues Festival in Greenville (Sept.), Seafood Festival Heritage Celebration in Biloxi (Sept.), Mississippi State Fair in Jackson (Oct.)

*1990 census

Natural resources: soil, water, trees, oil, natural gas, clay, sand and gravel, limestone, salt, bauxite, iron ore

Agricultural products: cotton, soybeans, peanuts, rice, wheat, chickens, eggs, beef cattle, dairy cattle

Manufactured goods: ships, motor vehicle parts, lighting equipment, stereos, telephones, food products, clothing, furniture, paper, fertilizers, plastics

ENDANGERED AND THREATENED SPECIES
Mammals—gray bat, Indiana bat, West Indian manatee, Florida panther
Birds—Mississippi sandhill crane, brown pelican, piping plover, wood stork, Bewick's wren
Reptiles—hawksbill turtle, leatherback turtle, gopher tortoise, ringed sawback turtle
Fish—bayou darter
Mussels—black clubshell, southern combshell, southern pink pigtoe, southern round pigtoe

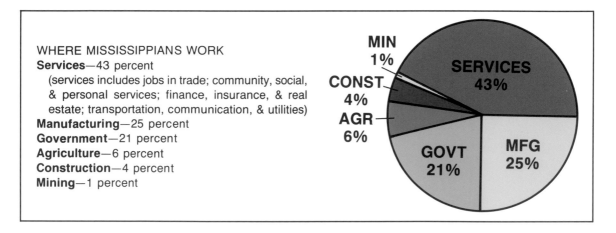

WHERE MISSISSIPPIANS WORK
Services—43 percent
(services includes jobs in trade; community, social, & personal services; finance, insurance, & real estate; transportation, communication, & utilities)
Manufacturing—25 percent
Government—21 percent
Agriculture—6 percent
Construction—4 percent
Mining—1 percent

Biloxi (buh-LUHK-see)

Chickasaw (CHIHK-uh-saw)

Choctaw (CHAHK-taw)

de Soto, Hernando (dih SOH-toh, hehr-NAHN-doh)

Hattiesburg (HAT-eez-burg)

La Salle, René-Robert Cavelier de (luh SAL, ruh-NAY-roh-BEHR ka-vuhl-yay duh)

Meridian (muh-RIHD-ee-uhn)

Natchez (NACH-ehz)

Pascagoula (pas-kuh-GOO-luh)

Tombigbee (tahm-BIHG-bee)

Yazoo (ya-ZOO)

Glossary

alluvium Clay, silt, sand, or gravel deposited by a river's running water. Areas where alluvium is found have very good soil for farming.

civil rights movement A movement to gain equal rights, or freedoms, for all citizens—regardless of race, religion, or sex.

delta A triangular piece of land at the mouth of a river. A delta is formed from soil deposited by the river.

dioxin A term that refers to a group of poisonous chemicals that contain carbon, oxygen, and chlorine. Dioxin is unintentionally produced when making various items, such as paper products and certain chemicals that kill weeds and insects. It can also be produced when many substances, such as wood or garbage, are burned. Deadly to some animals, dioxin can also cause health problems in humans.

plantation   A large estate, usually in a warm climate, on which crops are grown by workers who live on the estate. In the past, plantation owners usually used slave labor.

prairie   A large area of level or gently rolling grassy land with few trees.

Reconstruction   The period from 1865 to 1877 during which the U.S. government brought the Southern states back into the Union after the Civil War. Before rejoining the Union, a Southern state had to pass a law allowing black men to vote. Places destroyed in the war were rebuilt and industries were developed.

sharecropping   A system of farming large estates in which laborers, called sharecroppers, work the land in exchange for a share of the crop. Sharecroppers do not own the land, but they usually receive equipment and seeds from the landowner.

treaty   An agreement between two or more groups, usually having to do with peace or trade.

Index

Acknowledgments:

Maryland Cartographics, pp. 2, 10; Stephen Kirkpatrick, pp. 2–3, 8, 9, 11, 13, 14, 17, 52, 61, 71; George Karn, p. 7; Tennessee-Tombigbee Waterway Development Authority, pp. 15, 41, 47 (bottom right), 50; Dee Reed / Visuals Unlimited, p. 16; National Park Service, pp. 19 (inset), 26; © Gerald P. Smith / Laatsch-Hupp Photo, p. 12; © Barbara Laatsch-Hupp / Laatsch-Hupp Photo, pp. 19, 27, 48; © Henry J. Hupp / Laatsch-Hupp Photo, pp. 34, 47 (left); Independent Picture Service, pp. 20, 65 (top right); Library of Congress, pp. 22, 23, 65 (center right, bottom); Peabody Museum of Salem, p. 24; Woolaroc Museum, Bartlesville, Oklahoma, pp. 28–29; The Historic New Orleans Collection, Museum / Research Center, Acc. No. 1982.32.1, p. 30; Notman Photographic Archives, McCord Museum of Canadian History, p. 31; Old Court House Collections, Vicksburg, Mississippi, pp. 32–33; McCain Library and Archives. University Libraries. University of Southern Mississippi., p. 37; Bettmann, p. 38; University of Mississippi, p. 39; © Doug Bryant, D. Donne Bryant Stock, p. 42; Frederica Georgia, pp. 44, 53, 54 (inset), 56–57, 69; Lynda Richards, p. 43; Mississippi Department of Economic and Community Development, pp. 6, 45, 49; *Choctaw Community News*, p. 46; Choctaw Museum of the Southern Indian, p. 62 (center); NASA, p. 51; Mississippi Forestry Commission, p. 54; David L. Watts, Mississippi Outdoors, p. 58; Mississippi Department of Environmental Quality, p. 59; NAACP Public Relations, p. 62 (top left); Wilson F. Minor Papers, Special Collections Department, Mississippi State University Library, pp. 62 (top right), 65 (center left); Hollywood Book & Poster Co., pp. 62 (bottom right and left), 63 (top), 64 (top right, bottom left); Chicago Bears, p. 63 (center left); Pittsburgh Baseball Club, p. 63 (center right); Vernon J. Biever, p. 63 (bottom); Time Warner Enterprises, p. 64 (top left); Muddy Waters, Records Exclusively on Chess Records, p. 64 (bottom right); Harry Lingdon, p. 65 (top left); Jean Matheny, p. 66.